WHAT'S THE BIG DEAL ABOUT

Elections

WHAT'S THE BIG DEAL ABOUT

Elections

written by **Ruby Shamir**
illustrated by **Matt Faulkner**

PHILOMEL BOOKS

PHILOMEL BOOKS
An imprint of Penguin Random House LLC, New York

First published in picture book format by Philomel Books,
an imprint of Penguin Random House LLC, 2018.
Chapter book first published in the United States of America
by Philomel Books, an imprint of Penguin Random House LLC, 2020.

Text copyright © 2018, 2020 by Ruby Shamir.
Illustrations copyright © 2018, 2020 by Matt Faulkner.

THE LIBRARY OF CONGRESS HAS CATALOGED THE PICTURE BOOK EDITION AS FOLLOWS:
Names: Shamir, Ruby, author. | Faulkner, Matt, illustrator.
Title: What's the big deal about elections? / Ruby Shamir ; illustrated by Matt Faulkner. |
Description: New York, NY : Philomel Books, [2018] | Audience: Age 4–8. |
Audience: Grade 4 to 6. | Includes bibliographical references. | Identifiers: LCCN
2017028451 | ISBN 9781524738075 (hardcover) | ISBN 9781524738105 (e-book) |
Subjects: LCSH: Elections—United States—Juvenile literature. | Voting—United States—
Juvenile literature. | Suffrage—United States—Juvenile literature.
Classification: LCC JK1978 .S474 2018 | DDC 324.60973—dc23
LC record available at https://lccn.loc.gov/2017028451

HC ISBN 9780593116432
PB ISBN 9780593116401

Manufactured in China by
RR Donnelley Asia Printing Solutions Ltd.
1 3 5 7 9 10 8 6 4 2

Chapter book edited by Talia Benamy. Original picture book edited by Jill Santopolo.
Design by Jennifer Chung. Text set in Adobe Jenson Pro.

The art was created in three stages: first, thumbnail sketches—many small sketches
created for each illustration emphasizing page design, visual narrative, and light source; second,
intermediate sketches—several sketches created to refine the design of the book's characters
and their environment, details, etc.; and third, the final art, which was created with
watercolor and pencil on sanded Arches 140 lb. cold press paper.

To my favorite future voters:
Dante, Allegra, Romy, Immanuel, August,
Francisco, Ella, Eva, Eloise, Emilia, Theo, and Bea
—R.S.

In memory of my mom, Ruth Agnes Powers Faulkner
1928–2017
and for Kris, always
—M.F.

ONE PERSON, ONE VOTE

Picture the scene: Bonfires lighting up the town square as parades of brass bands march by. Floats wheeling caged raccoons, bears, and eagles before rowdy crowds. Torches exploding into shooting flames.

What was all the excitement about? It was Election Day the way Americans celebrated it about 200 years ago! Kids loved to be part of the action and couldn't wait until they were finally old enough to vote.

Life is very different these days, and Election Day looks pretty different too. But one thing remains the same—Americans still vote on Election Day. And when you're eighteen, you'll be able to vote too!

Why does that matter? What are Americans voting for and why is voting so important? What's the big deal about elections anyway?

In 1845, Election Day was set for the Tuesday after the first Monday of November. Why then? Many Americans were church-going farmers who lived far from the polls, so they couldn't go on Sunday but needed a full day to travel and be back home for Wednesday's market day. And November was after the busy harvesting season, but before the wintery weather made travel too difficult.

WHAT ARE
ELECTIONS?

Elections are a fair way to make decisions as a group. Say your class gets to choose what to play in gym, and ten kids say kickball, but only seven say tag. Well, kickball has won for that day. Every kid gets one vote, and the choice with the most votes wins.

Now, can you imagine getting to choose your teacher? Or your soccer coach? Or your parents? Elections are cool because we vote to choose the people in charge!

We elect our leaders to very big jobs—like president, governor, or mayor. That means those people get their power from us, the voters, who

DEMOCRACY

give those men and women those important positions. The US Constitution starts with the words "We the People" because we don't have a ruler who gets to be in charge forever. Instead, we decide together what's important and who's in charge. If they're not doing a good job, we get to choose new leaders in the next election.

One very big deal about elections is that "We the People" each get one vote. Doesn't matter if you're rich or poor, strong or scrawny, tall or short. Everyone has an equal say in the voting booth. Our government is elected to represent us!

In a running race, the fastest sprinter wins. In a spelling bee, the best speller wins. An election is a different kind of contest. The winner isn't necessarily the fastest or even the smartest, but the person who the most voters trust to be in charge and help them.

WHO GETS TO VOTE?

Most American citizens who are at least eighteen years old can vote where they live, but it wasn't always this way.

When the United States was first formed nearly 250 years ago, in most places only white men who owned a home or land were allowed to vote. No women, no African Americans, no Native Americans, no poor people, no one under the age of twenty-one—none of them had a say when the time came to pick leaders and representatives in government. Slowly, over many, many years, different groups of people demanded the right to vote, and they won.

Frederick Douglass knew that the right to vote in elections was an important part of American freedom. He demanded the vote for black Americans who were former slaves because "it is our right." He said that without the vote, "slavery is not abolished." Native Americans, the first people to live on this continent, were only granted American citizenship in 1924, and even then, it

took another forty years before every state allowed Native Americans to vote.

And even though kids like you can't vote yet, your voices still count. You can join with your friends and neighbors to stand up for what you believe in. When African Americans were denied the chance to participate in elections, children protested for the rights of their parents and grandparents. In so doing, they were marching for their very own futures too.

You have to be an American citizen to vote in most elections in this country. Anyone born in America is automatically a citizen. If you weren't born here, you can become a citizen, though it takes some time and effort.

We make change on Election Day with our votes, but we can make a difference every day through our actions.

Nearly fifty years ago, eighteen-year-olds won the right to vote. Before that, voters had to be twenty-one. Do you think kids younger than eighteen should be allowed to vote?

Kids who were brought to America very young but without the proper forms to be citizens are speaking up, declaring that they should be considered Americans because this is the only home they've ever known. They may not have the right to vote, but they have a voice and they demand to be heard.

WHY DO
WE VOTE?

We vote to elect people to lead the government. People who run for office are called candidates. Once candidates win elections, they're called elected officials, and they go to work in the government. But what exactly *is* the government?

For one thing, government is a way to organize, plan, and build things that are too big for one person or one family to do alone, especially things that we share, like roads.

We all need roads—to get to school, or to the store, or to the playground. But how do we decide where the road should go? Who will hire and

pay the workers to pave the road? What about lighting the road so people can use it at night? Who will make sure that everyone drives safely on the road?

Because we all share the road, we all should have a say in answering those questions—and we do! Through the people we elect, we get to decide what our government does. And to pay for big projects like roads, the government collects money—taxes—from all of us. One very important goal of voting is to have a say in how our tax money is spent. This was one of the reasons the American Revolution started, to tell the King of England he couldn't tax Americans "without representation," without giving them a say in English elections.

We all breathe the same air, right? A while back, cities and towns were often choked by smog from cars and factories that spewed out pollution. Americans were fed up with the dirty air and pushed for a law called the Clean Air Act of 1970, which helped clear the air. If we want these laws to stay in place, we have to elect people who care about clean air too!

Ever wonder why you have to go to school? By 1918, every state had passed a law that said that kids had to get an education. Before that time, many young kids had to work in dangerous factories or underground in dirty mines.

WHY DOES GOVERNMENT MATTER?

We live in a very big country. There are lots of things that happen every day that we don't even think about because the country seems to run on its own, but it doesn't.

Government workers include some of the most helpful people in our neighborhoods, like firefighters, police officers, and teachers. And elected officials in our government make decisions that touch our lives every day—not just in how to build roads, schools, and parks, but also how to pay the doctors and nurses who take care of us when we're sick, how to make sure our water is clean enough to drink, and how to keep our medicine and food safe. They make those decisions based on what we, the voters, think is important.

Garbage collection keeps the streets clean, waterways fresh, and our bodies healthy by clearing away germs. Before New York City's

Department of Sanitation—the world's biggest—was established, the city was so stinky that travelers could smell it from six miles away! In 1903, New Yorkers were so grateful for sanitation workers that they were cheered at a parade.

Choosing who serves in government is a very big deal!

If there's an emergency, call 911 on a phone and help will come speeding your way, no matter where you are in the country. A bunch of government offices partnered with phone companies to set up this special line. The very first 911 call was made from Haleyville, Alabama, in 1968.

WHO DO WE ELECT TO LEAD THE GOVERNMENT?

That depends on which government you're talking about.

The federal government, which is the one that oversees our whole country, is based in Washington, DC, and that's where the president and other leaders

live. But most elected officials stay right in your own state, or even in your city or town. While no two states are run exactly the same way, each is led by citizens who are elected by other citizens.

Governors and state representatives, mayors and city council members, county commissioners and even some local judges are elected to make sure everything close to home runs smoothly.

Would you believe that we have more than 90,000 state and local governments in the US? That's more governments than there are seats in a football stadium!

School board members are elected to make sure that public schools have healthy lunches, art supplies, sports equipment, caring teachers, and good principals. In many states, judges and sheriffs are elected too. There was even a time when towns would elect dogcatchers!

Who makes sure that playgrounds have safe equipment? How many firefighters can the city hire? Should there be a stop sign on that busy corner near your school? We elect state and local officials to make decisions and laws about these sorts of questions.

SO WHAT EXACTLY HAPPENS IN WASHINGTON, DC?

Washington, DC, is our nation's capital, the seat of government for the whole country, all 325 million of us living on almost 4 million square miles! The White House—the president's home and office—is there. We elect the president, who works with Congress to govern the nation.

The voters elect the president

The president nominates federal judges

Members of Congress are elected from every state, and they gather in Washington, DC, to make laws that matter for the entire country.

The House of Representatives and the Senate, the two chambers of Congress, write bills and pass them after debate. The president of the United States then signs those bills into law and carries them out.

The third branch of the federal government is the judiciary—judges—who help settle questions about the law. The president chooses federal judges and they're approved by the Senate. So while we don't directly elect those judges, they're selected and approved by people we elect.

The Senate confirms all federal judges

Different laws can be made for different cities and states, but the laws passed in Washington, DC, are about things that need to be the same all over the country. Like what? Well, from New York to New Mexico, we all need to have fresh water to drink. And from Colorado to Connecticut, we need clean air too. Whether you're in North Dakota or North Carolina, you should be able to use the same money. Congress also makes laws about when to go to war, how to make peace with other countries, and how to pay for everything by raising taxes.

Each of America's fifty states sends two senators to Washington, for a grand total of 100 senators. So even though California has tons more people than Alaska, they each have the same number of senators in Congress. But the House of Representatives has many more members—435 to be exact. States with more people living in them get to send more members to the House. Because of that, Alaska sends only one member to the House of Representatives and California sends fifty-three.

HOW DO WE ELECT OUR LEADERS?

It's usually pretty simple: we vote for the person we support, and the candidate with the most votes wins. This is how we elect pretty much all of our leaders. But presidential elections are different because we elect presidents through something called the Electoral College.

The Electoral College has nothing to do with the school you might go to after high school. Instead, it's a group of people from each state, called "electors." When we vote for president, we're actually voting for electors in our states, who will then turn around and vote for president. In most states, all of the electors of the state vote for the person who won the most votes in that state.

The number of electors is the number of House of Representatives members plus the number of senators, plus three for Washington, DC. States with more people have more electors in the Electoral College.

> The Electoral College system can be pretty confusing. There have been five presidential elections in our history where a candidate for president won more votes but didn't become president. Those candidates didn't win enough Electoral College votes.

1789 PRESIDENTIAL ELECTION

GEORGE WASHINGTON

HIS OPPONENT

George Washington was our first president and the only one elected who didn't run against anyone.

HOW DO WE KNOW WHO TO CHOOSE IN AN ELECTION?

It can be a tough choice! One way to choose is to listen to what candidates say they'll do and then make sure that they keep their promises after Election Day. We can do this by watching their debates, listening to their speeches, visiting their websites, and writing to them. If they don't keep their promises or do a good job, we can vote them out in the next election.

Another way is to learn what political party they're in. Sorry to say, political parties aren't anything like birthday parties—no cake, no candles, no gifts. Political parties are groups that people join because they agree on how the government should be run. And like when rooting for sports teams, people can get very excited about them.

In our country, we have two main political parties: the Democrats and the Republicans. How can such a big country, with so many people, have only two choices? We actually do have lots of smaller parties, but most voters choose candidates from one of the big two when they go to vote.

Democrats have a donkey as their symbol and Republicans have an elephant. Why? Each party got its animal symbol as a joke. When Democrat Andrew Jackson ran for president, he got called a donkey as an insult, but he didn't mind and slapped a picture of the animal onto his campaign posters. Republicans are elephants because a few newspaper cartoonists drew them that way and it stuck.

But the most important way to make a decision about who to vote for is to use your head and ask lots of questions. What's going on in your neighborhood? What should the government be doing that it isn't doing now? Is Congress passing good laws? How can the candidates who are running for office make a difference?

Even if the person you choose doesn't win, it's still important to vote, because it sends a message to the winner and others about what matters to you.

General elections in the US usually happen in November. But there are often other elections a few months before the big one, and they're called primaries and caucuses. In these contests, voters choose one person in each party who will be on the ballot on Election Day in November to run against the candidate the other party chooses.

WHO CAN RUN FOR OFFICE?

Anyone who is a citizen and old enough can run for office. Different positions have different requirements about how long you have to have been a citizen and where you need to live, but that's pretty much it for the rules.

To be president, you need to be at least thirty-five years old and be a natural-born US citizen. For the Senate, you have to be at least thirty years old, and for the House of Representatives, you need to be at least twenty-five. For both the Senate and the House of Representatives, you need to have been an American citizen for a while and live in the place you want to represent.

The presidency has attracted a wide range of candidates over the years. Belva Ann Lockwood ran for president nearly forty years before women had the right to vote, while Margaret Chase Smith was the first woman to be seriously considered for the presidency from one of the major political parties. Barack Obama was the first black American

1. Grover Cleveland 2. John Glenn 3. Aaron Burr
4. Gerald Ford 5. Henry Clay 6. Jesse Jackson
7. Shirley Chisholm 8. Alf Landon
9. Margaret Chase Smith

to win the presidency, but he wasn't the first African American to run. Jesse Jackson ran in 1988, and before that, in 1972, Shirley Chisholm was the first black woman to run for president. Her campaign slogan said she was "unbought and unbossed," and she worked hard to provide children with healthy food and doctors when they were sick.

10. Ted Kennedy   11. Al Smith   12. Adlai Stevenson
13. Belva Ann Lockwood   14. Millard Filmore
15. Barack Obama   16. Horace Greeley   17. Ross Perot
18. John Q. Adams

No matter your hairstyle, taste in food, fashion sense, favorite sport, or current job, you can be a candidate. Astronauts, actors, accountants, and more have all run for office!

How young can you be and hold office? One Pennsylvania town elected an eighteen-year-old to be mayor! His mom said he would still have to take out the garbage and keep the yard clear, though.

George Washington Albright was born a slave, but he overcame many obstacles and was eventually elected to public office. When Albright was a teenager, President Abraham Lincoln signed a proclamation to end slavery. Albright then joined a secret group and risked his life to sneak into neighboring slave quarters and announce that slavery was over. Years later, he was elected as a state senator in Mississippi.

HOW DO CANDIDATES GET ELECTED?

Running for office takes a lot of time and effort. Candidates meet as many voters as possible, listen to what's important to us, and talk about how they will stand up for us if they get elected. They meet voters at local festivals, hold large

VOTE TUESDAY NOV. 6TH

NO MORE STINKY POLLUTION!

GET OUT THE VOTE!

meetings, debate other candidates, and appear in the news. One popular stop for presidential candidates is the Iowa State Fair, where almost any food  you can imagine comes plopped on a stick: peanut butter and jelly, brownies, pork chops, salad, and even deep-fried butter! But to do all of this, candidates need help. That's where you come in.

Candidates will sometimes do strange things for a vote. In 1926, a candidate for mayor of Chicago brought a cage of rats onto a rally stage and yelled at them for a half hour, pretending they were his opponents. He went on to win his election.

Even as a kid, you can volunteer on a campaign and convince others to vote for your favorite candidate by making phone calls, knocking on your neighbors' doors, hanging up posters, handing out leaflets and campaign buttons, raising money, and speaking out about what you believe.

HOW DO
WE VOTE?

Every year on Election Day, citizens go to their polling places to vote, though every state has different rules for how it's done. Some places have voting machines where you touch a computer screen to record your vote, and in other states you fill out a paper ballot that gets fed into a counting machine.

These technologies are supposed to make voting quick, easy to count, and hard to cheat at. No new technology has been perfect, but we keep trying to come up with ways to make voting easier and more secure.

Before you can vote, though, you need to sign up, or register, to vote. This is another way you can get involved even before you're old enough to vote yourself—by encouraging all the grown-ups you know to register to vote so they can be ready to cast their ballots on Election Day.

Elections in early America often were rowdy and noisy. Sometimes voters would gather at the local town hall and simply yell out their choice or "stand by their man," the person who they wanted to win.

Even though we still have one Election Day in November, a lot of states offer other ways to vote: people can vote by mail and people can vote early—in some places a full month leading up to

Election Day. If you're away from home on Election Day, you can send in an absentee ballot. People serving overseas in the military can vote from where they're stationed. Even astronauts can vote from space!

WHAT HAPPENS AFTER ELECTIONS?

When candidates lose elections, they usually go home to their families and go on with their lives, though sometimes they choose to run for office again in the future. The winners, though, get to serve their term or terms in government.

When that term is up or they lose an election, an elected official willingly leaves office and hands his or her position over to the next person elected to that role. This is called the peaceful transfer of power, and strange as it sounds, it's a really big deal.

Election losers and elected officials whose

terms have ended don't start wars to take over the government, and they don't stay put and refuse to leave. They listen to the choice the voters made and move on, leaving the office to the next guy or gal who has been chosen by the will of the people.

The peaceful transfer of power shows that the real power isn't in the office or the elected official,

but in us, the voters. And that's why it's important to vote on Election Day and also stay active all year long, paying attention to what our leaders do and say, because in the end, we're in charge.

JUSTICE TAFT | REPRESENTATIVE ADAMS | PAINTER BUSH

Former presidents have stayed busy after they left office. Former President William H. Taft was appointed to serve on the Supreme Court, former President John Q. Adams was elected to the House of Representatives, and former President George W. Bush became a painter.

Elections are all about making sure the country is safe, prosperous, and fair well into the future. What do you think our government should spend its time on? What do you think our leaders should pay attention to?

TIMELINE

Colonial Period The right to vote varied in the colonies. Every colony required voters to own property or to pay a certain amount of taxes in order to be granted the right to vote. Some colonies barred Catholic or Jewish people from voting.

1787 The Constitution was written, establishing the supreme law of the land.

1788 Americans voted to approve, or ratify, the Constitution. Voting rights were determined by individual states, though in most places a voter had to be a white, male adult over twenty-one years old and own property.

1790 Vermont became the first state to grant voting rights to any free man; property-holding was not a requirement. All states eliminated religious tests and some allowed free African Americans to vote.

1807 Women who owned property were allowed to vote in New Jersey until 1807 when New Jersey outlawed women's voting rights.

1845 The US Congress established Election Day as the Tuesday after the first Monday of November.

1869 Wyoming became the first state or territory to grant women over age twenty-one the right to vote.

1870 The Fifteenth Amendment to the Constitution was ratified, granting African American men the right to vote.

1888 Massachusetts became the first state to pass a law establishing a voting system with secret ballots printed by the government.

1920 The Nineteenth Amendment to the Constitution was ratified, granting women the right to vote.

1924 The Indian Citizenship Act was signed, granting American citizenship to Native Americans.

1926 Throughout early American history, many states and territories had allowed new immigrants who were noncitizens to vote. Arkansas was the last state to ban noncitizen voting in 1926.

1965 The Voting Rights Act was signed, outlawing unfair barriers that stopped citizens, particularly African Americans, from voting.

1971 The Twenty-sixth Amendment was ratified, granting citizens eighteen years and older the right to vote.

AUTHOR'S NOTE

Elections are about power, and choosing who is in power matters. I wrote this book to show children that they wield power, and how they use it is precious. Elections are an exercise in civic participation that give ordinary people a say about who their leaders are and how we want our communities to operate. If more of us are involved in the electoral process, we will inevitably elect people to office who better reflect the communities we want to build. The time we spend learning about issues that matter to our communities, and to our country, is valuable. The effort we make supporting candidates is meaningful. The votes we cast matter. And our continued engagement to hold elected officials accountable keeps our communities vibrant. We all have agency, and I hope this book gives kids a glimpse of how to use theirs.

I relied on a lot of wonderful sources as I did the research for this book, including the official White House website and the website of the Library of

Congress. Below are several of the insightful books I used as resources:

- ★ *You're More Powerful Than You Think: A Citizen's Guide to Making Change Happen,* by Eric Liu
- ★ *The Virgin Vote: How Young Americans Made Democracy Social, Politics Personal, and Voting Popular in the Nineteenth Century,* by Jon Grinspan
- ★ *Give Me Liberty!: An American History,* by Eric Foner
- ★ *Marching for Freedom: Walk Together, Children, and Don't You Grow Weary,* by Elizabeth Partridge
- ★ *The Everything American Government Book: From the Constitution to Present-Day Elections, All You Need to Understand Our Democratic System,* by Nick Ragone
- ★ *Deliver the Vote: A History of Election Fraud, an American Political Tradition—1742–2004,* by Tracy Campbell
- ★ *Party Politics in America,* by Marjorie Randon Hershey
- ★ *The Fight to Vote,* by Michael Waldman

Don't miss the other fun and fact-filled books in this series!

WHAT'S THE BIG DEAL ABOUT

Freedom

Ruby Shamir ⋆ Matt Faulkner

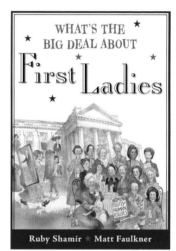

WHAT'S THE BIG DEAL ABOUT

First Ladies

Ruby Shamir ⋆ Matt Faulkner

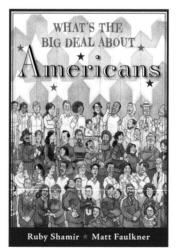

WHAT'S THE BIG DEAL ABOUT

Americans

Ruby Shamir ⋆ Matt Faulkner